T

xodus

The Regathering of the Children of Israel Is God's Plan for the Last Days.

The Final Exodus

The Regathering of the Children of Israel Is God's Plan for the Last Days.

William Carr Blood

The Final Exodus

Published by:

McDougal Publishing
P.O. Box 3595
Hagerstown, MD 21742
www.mcdougalpublishing.com

ISBN 1-58158-084-3

Printed in the United States of America
For Worldwide Distribution

Library of Congress Catalog Card Number: 99-66102

Dedication

To

The innumerable multitude
of the children of Israel.
God "will make them one nation
in the land,
on the mountains of Israel."

(Ezekiel 37:22)

Appreciation

The value of my wife's partnership in preparing this book is impossible to acknowledge or commend with words. Dorothy's discernment and wisdom improved the text to be more understandable for readers of any inclination. Only a wife dedicated to God and her husband would have persevered in perfectionism on our word processor during the many late hours. She is truly a "gift from God," which is the meaning of her name.

"A prudent wife is from the LORD."
(Proverbs 19:14)

Memorial

Albert Houston Chubb (1931-1995)

Al Chubb was founder of Radio Station WAJL in Winter Park, Florida. His love for Israel and material investment in the **"Glorious Land"** was an inspiring demonstration of what God wants all His people to achieve.

On my first visit to Israel, I joined Al's "Bless Israel" Holy Land Tour. His resounding singing voice was accentuated by the perfect acoustics of St. Anne's Church. He received standing ovations as he sang in the open-air amphitheater at Caesarea. These are the memories that will never fade. Nor will the feeling of being "home" as I deplaned at the Tel Aviv Airport be erased from my memory. These joyful emotions were sustained by Al's humble exuberance and evening teachings in the hotel. I am forever grateful for his friendship and example of love for God's chosen people.

❖◆❖

"The memory of the righteous is blessed."
(Proverbs 10:7)

Aliyah!

Aliyah is a Hebrew word for "ascension" or to "go up" or "move up" to Israel. People who immigrate to Israel are known as *olim* (plural), *oleh* (male) or *olah* (female), referring to those who *"come up" to Jerusalem.*

The Northern Kingdom of Israel was defeated and deported by the Assyrians in 721 B.C. The Southern Kingdom of Judah and its capital Jerusalem were captured by the Babylonians, who took most of the survivors to Babylon between 605 and 586 B.C. After seventy years in captivity, remnants of the Southern Kingdom were released by King Cyrus of Persia, who encouraged them to ***"go up to Jerusalem...and build the house of the LORD God of Israel."*** (Ezra 1:3)

The Roman Empire defeated Israel and most of the population was dispersed throughout the known world between A.D. 66 and 135. Jewish refugees fleeing poverty and persecution in the former Soviet Union began immigrating to the Holy Land in 1882. These and following *Aliyah* movements are responsible for Israel's development as a world power. Three million *olim*, representing twenty percent of the world's Jewish population, went *up to Jerusalem* during the past century. The largest groups were survivors of the Holocaust after World War II in 1945, and people from the former Soviet Union following the collapse of Communism in 1989.

Persons obtaining an immigration visa to Israel may be provided transportation from their country of residence to Israel. *Olim* may also qualify for government assistance programs for their first year in Israel. These may include home mortgage loans or rental grants, medical insurance, Hebrew language classes, subsistence allowances, job training and employment, children's schooling and individual preparations for higher education.

Since 1948, Jewish people have had their own country where they can live and where they are wanted. Their government is making every effort to welcome them and help them to begin a new life in the land God promised them four thousand years ago.

Contents

Introduction

One of my high school part-time jobs was ushering at the Rialto Theater, the only movie house in East Rochester, New York. World War II dominated the Movietone News preceding the feature movies and I was shocked to see the Holocaust concentration camps and their emaciated survivors. The unthinkable atrocities were overshadowed only by the staggering numbers of people killed or made homeless.

Years later, I visited the first concentration camp at Dachau, Germany. It was a vivid reminder that these horrible actions were planned and conducted by and against people of my generation and in my lifetime. Elie Wiesel, a youthful survivor who became a Nobel laureate in 1986 and wrote the worldwide best-selling book *Night*, is only a few months younger than I. Oskar Schindler, who saved over one thousand Jewish workers, was about my father's age. Corrie ten Boom, a survivor whose story was told in the movie *The Hiding Place*, was sheltering Jewish refugees in her Holland home during my tenure at the Rialto.

In 1984, Seymour "Cy" Verbin gave me the book *Exodus II* by Steve Lightle. My friend's smiling comment was, "I believe God wants you to have this." While lacking knowledge in Bible prophecy, I was intrigued by the author's 1974 prophetic vision of the Jewish population in Russia moving to Israel. In 1996, Ginny Schlensker, an inspiring woman of God, encouraged me to study the biblical history of Israel. Many months later, I joined these two friends in understanding the greatest human experience, ***participation in the fulfillment of prophecy!*** This book, *The Final Exodus*, has been translated into Russian and Spanish for use by organizations helping the immigrants make their *Aliyah* journey to Israel.

Every time an American volunteer helps a Jewish mother carry her young son aboard the Russian passenger ship to carry immigrants from the Ukraine to Israel, they are doing what the prophet Isaiah spoke during the reign of King Hezekiah in 712 B.C. (See page 87.)

> **"They** (the Gentiles–American volunteers) **shall bring your sons in their arms."**
> (Isaiah 49:22)

The regathering of people to Israel is **THE FINAL EXODUS** and continuing proof that the Bible is true.

William Carr Blood

PART 1

The People of God

"And who is like Your people, like Israel, the one nation on the earth whom God went to redeem for Himself as a people, to make for Himself a name....For You have made Your people Israel Your very own people forever; and You, LORD, have become their God."

(2 Samuel 7:23, 24)

CHAPTER 1

The Plan

When God told Moses to tell the Israelites, **"God has chosen you to be a people for Himself, a special treasure above all the peoples on the face of the earth,"**...and that He said, **"I will take you as My people, and I will be your God,"** all the children of Israel became His chosen people, **"The Holy People,"** forever. A distinctly different people, **"the people** (children of Israel) **shall dwell alone, and shall not be reckoned among the nations** (Gentiles)," to show the world that Israel's God is the only true God. This unique relationship is essential in God's plan of salvation for the world. (Exodus 6:7; Numbers 23:9, KJV; Deuteronomy 7:6; Isaiah 62:12)

Many Gentiles consider themselves to be Christians, but a more accurate name would be Judeo-Christians because their relationship with God is rooted in Judaism.

The apostle Paul clarified this when he spoke about his brethren and kinsmen, the Israelites:

"...to whom pertain the adoption (by God as a nation), **the glory** (visible, continuing manifestation of God's presence in the wilderness), **the covenants, the giving of the law** (Law of Moses–the Torah), **the service of God** (divine order of worship with provision for the forgiveness of sin), **and the promises."** (Romans 9:4)

Our debt to the Jewish people cannot be calculated. They are the source of the patriarchs, prophets, apostles, Bible and Jesus. They use the same book, the Tanakh, which Gentiles call the Old Testament. The Tanakh was written by men who experienced miracles, saw visions, had dreams, talked with angels, heard the voice of God, and were guided by the Holy Spirit. They recorded their experiences on crude scrolls that were carefully preserved and copied by generations of Israelites. We are told how they **"having seen the promises afar off were assured of them, embraced them and confessed that they were strangers and pilgrims on the earth."** God did this so we could read the Bible and learn what is happening. (Hebrews 11:13)

Jesus was born Jewish. We are bonded to God's chosen people by having the same God, the same Messiah and the same Holy Spirit. Every calendar reminds us of His birth and life: A.D. 2006 means, "Anno Domini (in the year of the Lord) 2006." Without Him we would not have the foundation for our families, education, hospitals, government, civil liberties and human rights found in the Bible. We are grateful for our Judeo-Christian heritage that is responsible for our existence and well-being, **"having been built on the foundation of the apostles and prophets."** (Ephesians 2:20)

These blessings have come upon us because God selected a childless man named Abraham and his barren wife, Sarah, to birth a new race of people. They would be **"His own special people,...a holy nation,...for renown, for praise, and for glory...the apple of His eye"** for the purpose of making known to **"the wickedness of man"** that there is a sovereign and loving God. (Genesis 6:5; Jeremiah 13:11; Zechariah 2:8; 1 Peter 2:9)

God told Israel, **"You are My witnesses...that I am God....The Gentiles shall come to your light."** He proves His existence in times of Israel's obedience: **"Those who honor Me I will honor....Blessings shall come upon you...because you obey the voice of the LORD...in the land which the LORD your God is giving you,"** and disobedience: **"Those who despise Me will be lightly esteemed....Your sins have withheld good from you...and limited the Holy One of Israel...because you did not serve the LORD."** These actions demonstrate God's promises to reward obedience and withhold blessings to punish disobedience. (Deuteronomy 28:2, 8, 47; 1 Samuel 2:30; Psalm 78:41, KJV; Isaiah 43:10-12; 60:3; Jeremiah 5:25)

God **"declared His word to Israel....To them were committed the oracles of God....Moses wrote all**

the words of the LORD." God told Jeremiah, **"Write in a book for yourself all the words that I have spoken to you,"** and told the apostle John, **"What you see, write in a book."** (Exodus 24:4; Psalm 147:19; Jeremiah 30:2; Romans 3:2; Revelation 1:11)

King David wrote that Israel was to **"Proclaim the good news of His** (God's) **salvation from day to day,...His glory among the nations** (Gentiles). **...Make known His deeds among the peoples! ...Talk of all His wondrous works!"** Other prophets wrote, **"I know that my Redeemer** (God) **lives....The LORD redeems the soul of His servants,...will forgive their iniquity, and...will remember their sin no more....Your dead shall live....Those who sleep in the dust of the earth shall awake...to everlasting life...at the end of the days....None of those who trust in Him shall be condemned."**
(1 Chronicles 16:8, 9, 23, 24; Job 19:25; Psalm 34:22; Isaiah 26:19; Jeremiah 31:34; Daniel 12:2, 13)

God's plan is unfolding hour by hour as written by the prophet Ezekiel:

"Thus says the Lord GOD: 'Surely I will take the children of Israel from among the nations (Gentiles), **wherever they have gone, and will gather them from every side and bring them into their own land; and I will make them one nation in the land, on the mountains of Israel.... The nations** (Gentiles) **also will know that I, the LORD, sanctify** (set apart as sacred and holy) **Israel.' "** (Ezekiel 37: 21-22, 28)

CHAPTER 2

The Chosen People

To accomplish His plan, **"God at the first visited the Gentiles to take out of them a people for His name."** God chose **"Abraham from the other side of the River** (Euphrates)**...and gave him Isaac.... Isaac begot Jacob, and...Jacob** (renamed Israel) **and his children went down to Egypt."** Moses, the first prophet to the Nation of Israel, led the children of Israel out of Egypt and through the wilderness for forty years. It was there that they were transformed into a nation under God's laws. (Joshua 24:3, 4; Matthew 1:2; Acts 15:14)

After Moses died, Joshua led the Nation of Israel into the Promised Land. Joshua died, and **"When all that generation had been gathered to their fathers, another generation arose after them who did not know the LORD nor the work which He had done for Israel."** As a result, national leadership and the worship of God, declined until **"the LORD raised up judges"** to help them. Samuel was judging Israel when the people asked for **"a king to judge us like all the nations."** (Judges 2:10, 16; 1 Samuel 8:5)

God chose Saul to be their first king. King David was next, and he expanded Israel into a powerful nation. After his death, his son King Solomon built the first temple for the worship of God. During the reigns of David and Solomon, the land occupied by Israel, or subject to it by treaty, included all the land God had promised them.[1]

Solomon's son Rehoboam, the fourth king, caused the country to be divided into two nations. Israel, consisting of ten tribes, was known as the Northern Kingdom, with its capital in Samaria. The tribes of Judah and Benjamin formed the Southern Kingdom of Judah around Jerusalem.

All the kings of Israel refused to honor God, and the nation was defeated by Assyria around 722 B.C. Most of the people were deported to Assyria and assimilated into that population. Judah had several kings who honored God, but their influence was not lasting. Jerusalem and the first temple were destroyed by the Babylonians between 605 and 586 B.C., and all but the poor people went into captivity in Babylon.

About 536 B.C., a remnant of Judah returned to Jerusalem to build the second temple and re-establish the Nation of Israel, which survived until the Romans destroyed Jerusalem in A.D. 70 and dispersed most of the people among several countries. Jesus of Nazareth was born about 4 B.C. and **"began His ministry at about thirty years of age."** (Luke 3:23)

In 1948, following actions by the United Nations, the Nation of Israel was re-established a second time in a small portion of the Holy Land. In the past fifty years, it has become a world power and the center of international attention while being one of the smallest countries on the globe with only six million of the world's less than fourteen million total Jewish population living within its borders.

During the 1,878 years between A.D. 70 and 1948, the Jews were a people without a country but they maintained their Jewish identity and religion. They fulfilled the prophecy that:

> **"The Gentiles shall know that the house of Israel went into captivity for their iniquity; because they were unfaithful to Me** (God), **...I gave them into the hand of their enemies."** (Ezekiel 39:23)

Those who returned to Israel in 1948 fulfilled other prophecies:

> **"You** (God) **will arise and have mercy on Zion; for the time to favor her, yes, *the set time, has come.*"** (Psalm 102:13)

> **"Now I will bring back the captives of Jacob, and have mercy on the whole house**

> **of Israel;...and I will make them one nation in the land, on the mountains of Israel....The Lord your God will bless you in the land...I do not do this for your** (Israel's) **sake....It is not because of your righteousness or the uprightness of your heart...but for My holy name's sake....The nations shall know that I am the Lord...when I am hallowed in you before their eyes."** (Deuteronomy 9:5; 30:16; Ezekiel 36:22-23; 37:22; 39:25)

When the Hebrew prophets recorded the words of God, they wrote their own past, present and future history which has been and continues to be living proof that everything in the Bible is true.

Hebrews and Jews

Abraham was called **"the Hebrew,"** probably meaning he had lived on **"the other side of the** (Euphrates) **River"** before moving to the Holy Land. The children of Israel were called **"Hebrews"** until the seventy-year Babylonian captivity. After returning to Jerusalem, they were more commonly called **"Jews,"** a name derived from the tribe of Judah which ruled the Southern Kingdom of Judah from Jerusalem before the captivity. (Genesis 14:13; Exodus 3:18; Joshua 24:3; Ezra 5:1)

PART 2

The Holy Land

"The LORD made a covenant with Abram, saying: 'To your descendants I have given this land, from the river of Egypt to the great river, the River Euphrates.' " (Genesis 15:18)

(The **"river of Egypt"** is known as the Wadi el-Arish located south of Gaza on the Mediterranean Sea.)

CHAPTER 3

The Promised Land

"In the beginning God created the heavens and the earth." He told Moses, **"All the earth is Mine."** However, Israel is the only place on earth that God called **"My land,"** and named Himself **"the Creator of Israel"** and **"King of Israel."** Israel is the only country founded by a divine promise and sovereign act of God. It is **"the one nation on the earth whom God went to redeem for Himself as a people,...a land that I** (God) **had searched out for them,...the glory of all lands.... The eyes of the LORD your God are always on it.... I** (God) **will plant them in their land, and no longer shall they be pulled up from the land I have given them.... They shall inherit the land forever."** Israel is called the **"Holy Land," "Glorious Land," "glorious kingdom"** and **"glorious holy mountain."** *It is wisdom to watch Israel for prophetic fulfillment of*

God's plan for the world. (Genesis 1:1; Exodus 19:5; Deuteronomy 11:12; 2 Samuel 7:23; Isaiah 43:15; 44:6; 60:21; Ezekiel 20:6; 38:16; Daniel 11:16, 20, 45; Amos 9:15; Zechariah 2:12)

Israel is truly a unique land. The 9,232-foot Mount Hermon on the northern border has ski slopes comparable to the Swiss Alps. The Dead Sea along the southern border is 1,312 feet below sea level and the lowest point on the earth's surface. The country is approximately 260 miles long and 70 miles wide, slightly smaller than the State of New Jersey. However, this is only a small portion of the land given to them by God. Jerusalem, the capital of Israel, is one of the oldest continuously occupied cities in the world. Israel has a Jewish population of about six million and produces 95 percent of its own food.[1] **"I** (God) **will raise up for them a garden of renown, and they shall...fill the face of the world with fruit** (exports)**."** (Isaiah 27:6; Ezekiel 34:29)

The official languages are Hebrew and Arabic. Hebrew, revived as a spoken language a century ago, is the only ancient language to have fallen out of verbal usage and then experience a complete resurgence in modern times.[2] **"I** (God) **will restore to the peoples a pure language."** (Zephaniah 3:9)

Four thousand years ago, the Promised Land was the major crossroads of international trade routes connecting Africa, Asia and Europe. God planted His people so travelers from other nations could see how *they lived and prospered in Israel* when they worshiped Him and lived by His laws. His plan was that visitors would return to their home countries and say, **"Surely this great nation is a wise and understanding people....Then the nations shall know that I am the LORD, the Holy One in Israel."** This proved true when the Queen of Sheba traveled from Ethiopia to visit King Solomon in Jerusalem. At the end of her visit, she said, **"Blessed be the LORD your God, who...has loved Israel forever."** (Deuteronomy 4:6; 1 Kings 10:9; Ezekiel 39:7)

It has also proven true in our time. Since 1948, they have rebuilt and worked the formerly desolate land of Israel so that today products and produce are exported all over the world. **"So they will say, 'This land that was desolate has become like the garden of Eden.'... Then the nations which are left all around you shall know that I, the LORD, have rebuilt the ruined places and planted what was desolate....*The LORD your God will bless you in the land.*"** (Deuteronomy 30:16; Ezekiel 36:35, 36)

God chose Abraham to be the father of a new nation of people. In His covenants with Abraham, Isaac and Jacob, God assured them their descendants would have the land **"from the river of Egypt to the great river, the River Euphrates,"** and **"the land on which you** (Jacob) **lie I** (God) **will give to you and your descendants."** These were clearly unconditional and everlasting covenants. (Genesis 15:18; 28:13)

The children of Israel followed Joshua into the Promised Land about 1422 B.C. They divided it among their tribes and remained there until about 586 B.C. when the Babylonians captured Jerusalem and deported most of the population to Babylon. A remnant of people from the nation of Judah returned to Jerusalem about 536 B.C. to rebuild the temple and re-establish the nation. They remained in the land until the Romans destroyed Jerusalem in A.D. 70. In 1948, the State of Israel was re-established the second time under a United Nations resolution, and God has declared that **"they shall inherit the land forever."** (Isaiah 60:21)

The descendants of Jacob (Israel) lived in the Promised Land as a family before going to Egypt and have had a continuous presence in the land since about 1422 B.C. Some people were not deported to Babylon and their families were still there when the second temple was built. The Romans deported Jewish survivors after capturing Jerusalem, but many remained and others returned between A.D. 70 and 1948 and they are still returning. No other people emanating from one family have lived continuously in their designated homeland for over 3,428 years (1422 + 2006), while maintaining their national identity, ancient language, religion and culture. Only Israel has done this.

Years after making unconditional and everlasting covenants with Abraham, Isaac and Jacob, God said, **"My covenant I will not break, nor alter the word that has gone out of My lips.... For I am the Lord, I do not change."** God said His people would return to Israel as a nation, and they are doing it! (Psalm 89:34; Malachi 3:6)

CHAPTER 4

Sarah's Only Son

Thousands of Arabs and Moslems want to live peacefully as citizens of Israel. However, when the State of Israel was re-established in 1948, radical Islamic Fundamentalists of Arab and Moslem nations in and around the Holy Land increased worldwide oil-based economic pressures. They used deception diplomacy, historical revisionism, Holocaust denial, terrorist aggression and military warfare (1948, 1956, 1967 and 1973) designed to destroy the Jewish nation. The late Yasir Arafat, leader of the Palestine Liberation Organization (PLO), stated, "Our objective is the destruction of Israel."[1] Their intention is to convert all people to the Islamic faith by any means. This defective mentality is the motivation for Islamic terrorism throughout the world. God has told us, **"Thus they have despised My people, as if they should no more be a nation before them."** (Jeremiah 33:24)

Some Arabs wrongly claim rights to Israel's Promised Land as descendants of Abraham, Ishmael and Esau. Ishmael was Isaac's older half brother, born to Sarah's **"Egyptian maidservant...Hagar."** Esau was Jacob's (renamed Israel) twin brother. However, God promised Abraham, **"Sarah your wife shall bear you a son, and you shall call his name Isaac; I will establish My covenant with him for an everlasting covenant, and with his descendants after him."**
(Genesis 16:1; 17:19)

Sarah's first and only child, Isaac, was born the following year and she told Abraham, **"The son** (Ishmael) **of this bondwoman shall not be heir with my son** (Isaac)**."** God then reconfirmed what He had said previously, **"Whatever Sarah has said to you** (Abraham)**, listen to her voice; for in Isaac your seed shall be called."** God later told Abraham three times that Isaac is **"your only son."**
(Genesis 21:10, 12; 22:2, 12, 16)

God also told Moses, **"Thus you shall say to the children of Israel: 'The LORD God of your fathers, the God of Abraham, the God of Isaac, and the God of Jacob** (Israel)**, has sent me to you.' "** (Exodus 3:15)

Scripture clearly records how God unconditionally promised the land of Israel as an everlasting possession to the descendants of Abraham, Isaac and Jacob. Anyone else desiring this land can only base their claim on political considerations, **"but...have no heritage or right or memorial in Jerusalem."** (Nehemiah 2:20) (Also see "Liberation Theology" on page 56.)

PART 3

Warning

"I am making known to you what shall happen in the latter time...; for at the appointed time the end shall be."

(Daniel 8:19)

CHAPTER 5

The Flood

God's chosen people have been involved in many "Exodus" movements to escape anti-Semitic forces or God's judgment on the land where they were living. Noah led his family on the most important Exodus. They escaped God's judgment of the earth by the Great Flood, and from this one family **"the whole earth was populated."** (Genesis 9:19)

> **"By faith Noah, being divinely warned of things not yet seen, moved with godly fear, prepared an ark for the saving of his household."** (Hebrews 11:7)

God warned Noah, giving him a relocation plan with the ark. Everyone who did not escape with him perished when **"the flood came and destroyed them all."** This three-step progression of ***WARNING,***

RELOCATION and ***PERSECUTION*** has occurred many times since the Great Flood. (Luke 17:27)

The most documented persecution of Jewish people occurred during the Holocaust from 1933 through 1945. Years earlier, Jewish leaders traveled throughout Europe warning their people to move to the land of Israel. Those who did not were persecuted, killed or went into hiding during the Holocaust.

The Holocaust is the most shocking, incomprehensible event in European history. Following orders of Adolf Hitler, the German government deliberately and systematically murdered over twelve million civilian men, women and children. They included Christian leaders and church members, elderly and handicapped people, infants and children, political opponents and anyone who disagreed with the government.

The largest single group of people killed was six million Jews including one-and-a-half million children. Their only "crime" was being Jewish. In the years before being murdered, they were prohibited from leaving their country, declared to be inferior to the German people, falsely accused and ridiculed in the media, refused public education and employment, denied due legal process, and required to wear a Star of David on their clothing.

Next came forced segregation into ghettos, burning of synagogues, and destruction or confiscation of property.

Following these humiliations, they were imprisoned in concentration camps to work at forced labor or sent to extermination camps to be murdered in poison gas chambers and their bodies incinerated.

This calculated genocide caused the death of one third of the Jewish people of the world. It is defined by the word *Holocaust*, which according to the dictionary means, "an offering which is completely burned."[1]

Throughout those years, thousands rushed to leave Europe using false identification documents or evaded border guards to escape persecution. Others hid in small living spaces in homes or farms of compassionate families. Some assumed other identities and lived as non-Jewish persons. Many gave their children to strangers who reared them until the war ended. Groups of partisans also lived in the countryside and conducted guerrilla warfare against German military forces. Thousands more survived the ghettos and inhumane conditions of concentration camps to become part of the ten million homeless and displaced persons in Europe when World War II ended in 1945.

As you read this, anti-Semitism is continuing in many countries including the United States. Gentile "hate groups" and Moslem extremists are desecrating Jewish cemeteries, vandalizing and burning synagogues, and abusing Jewish individuals verbally and physically. They are also trying to convince the world that the

Holocaust never occurred, even though it has been extensively documented for more than fifty years and has thousands of survivors and living witnesses.

Men of God are warning people today just as they did in Europe seventy years ago. The message is the same as what God spoke to Jacob, **"Return to the land of your fathers."** (Genesis 31:3)

CHAPTER 6

Escape for Your Life

There are many examples of God showing His love for His people by ***WARNING*** them to *escape His judgment of Gentile nations:*

> **"Surely the Lord GOD does nothing, unless He reveals His secret to His servants the prophets."** (Amos 3:7)

Angels warned Lot to escape God's judgment of Sodom and Gomorrah:

> **"Escape for your life!...lest you be destroyed."** (Genesis 19:17)

Jeremiah warned his people living in Babylon to leave before it was conquered by the Medes:

> **"Flee from the midst of Babylon,**
> **and every one save his life!**

> **Do not be cut off in her iniquity,**
> **for this is the time of the LORD's vengeance."**
> (Jeremiah 51:6)

Warnings may be confirmed by world events and attitudes of people:

> **"You will hear of wars and rumors of wars.... There will be famines, pestilences** (epidemics), **and earthquakes,...a destroying storm,...the sea and the waves roaring,...flooding rain,...great hailstones,...fire and pillars of smoke, ...scorching,...fiery lightning,...waters harden** (frozen) **like stone,...prolonged plagues** (AIDS)**...which cannot be healed."** (Deuteronomy 28:22, 35, 59; Job 38:30; Psalm 78:48; Isaiah 28:2; Ezekiel 13:11; Joel 2:30; Matthew 24:6, 7; Luke 21:25)

> **"They revile and persecute you, and say all kinds of evil against you falsely."** (Matthew 5:11)

> **"People have spoken, saying, 'The two families** (Judah and Israel) **which the LORD has chosen, He** (God) **has also cast them off.'... Thus they have despised My people."** (Jeremiah 33:24) (See page 57.)

Some people may not understand or believe a warning. This was a fatal mistake for Lot's sons-in-law:

> **"To his sons-in-law he seemed to be joking."** (Genesis 19:14)

Personal prosperity and comforts of living outside

Israel influence people who do not relocate. When Jeremiah told the refugees of Jerusalem to return to Judah from Egypt, the people responded:

> **"We will not listen to you! We will certainly do…as we have done, we and our fathers…. Then we had plenty of food, were well off, and saw no trouble."** (Jeremiah 44:16, 17)

Warnings ultimately guide God's chosen people to Israel where He can fulfill His plan and purpose for their lives. These plans are well defined throughout Scripture:

> **"There is a God in heaven who reveals secrets, and He has made known…what will be in the latter days."** (Daniel 2:28)

> "It shall come to pass in that day **that the Lord shall set His hand *again the second time* to recover the remnant of His people who are left…. He will set up a banner for the nations, and will assemble the outcasts of Israel, and gather together the dispersed of Judah from the four corners of the earth."** (Isaiah 11:11, 12)

> **" 'Behold, I will send for many fishermen,' says the LORD, 'and they shall fish them; and afterward I will send for many hunters, and they shall hunt them from every mountain and every hill, and out of the holes of the rocks.' "** (Jeremiah 16:16)
> **"Then you will know that I am the LORD,**

when I bring you into the land of Israel.... And I will make them one nation in the land, on the mountains of Israel."
(Ezekiel 20:42; 37:22)

"They shall inherit the land forever.... I will plant them in their land, and they shall no more be pulled up out of their land which I have given them."
(Isaiah 60:21; Amos 9:15, KJV)

"*The* Lord *your God will bless you in the land which you go to possess*.... For I know the thoughts that I think toward you, says the Lord, thoughts of peace and not of evil, to give you a future and a hope."
(Deuteronomy 30:16; Jeremiah 29:11)

"*Again I will build you, and you shall be rebuilt.* ... I will put My Spirit within you.... Then they shall know that I am the Lord."
(Jeremiah 31:4; Ezekiel 36:27, 38)

When Isaiah said, **"The Lord shall set His hand *again the second time* to recover the remnant of His people...from the four corners of the earth,"** he foretold the return of Jewish exiles **"*again* from all the nations"** where they were **"scattered"** after Jerusalem was destroyed in A.D. 70. The "first" return would be the two tribes held captive 70 years in one nation (Babylon) that returned to Jerusalem in 536 B.C. (Deuteronomy 30:3; Isaiah 11:11, 12)

"Then the heads of the fathers' houses of Judah and Benjamin (in Babylon)**,...with all**

> **whose spirits God had moved, arose to go up and build the house of the LORD which is in Jerusalem."** (Ezra 1:5)

Seventeen years after the captives returned to Jerusalem from Babylon, Zechariah also foretold the second return. This started in 1882 when refugees fleeing persecution in Russia came to the Holy Land.

> **"I** (God) **will save My people from the land of the east,...the west,...Egypt,...Assyria,.... And they shall dwell in the midst of Jerusalem."** (Zechariah 8:7, 8; 10:10)

The **"fishermen"** and **"hunters"** are Gentiles looking for God's people in foreign nations and helping them move to Israel. (Jeremiah 16:16) (See pages 87-90.)

> They **"seek out My sheep and deliver them from all the places where they were scattered."... They** (fishermen) **read distinctly from the book** (Old Testament)**...and helped them** (Jewish refugees) **to understand...the words of the LORD.... 'Return to the land of your fathers.' Then they shall bring all your brethren...out of all nations...one by one...to My holy mountain Jerusalem."** (Genesis 31:3; Nehemiah 8:8; Isaiah 27:12; 66:20; Jeremiah 36:8; Ezekiel 34:12)

These **"fishermen"** and **"hunters"** were not needed in the return to Jerusalem from Babylon.

> **"Thus says Cyrus king of Persia:...Go up to Jerusalem...and build the house of the**

> **Lord God of Israel."** (Ezra 1:2, 3)

Ezekiel states that they would return to the **"land of Israel"** where God will make them a **"nation."** On May 14, 1948, the Nation of Israel was re-established in one day. This was the greatest fulfillment of prophecy in almost 2,000 years![1] (Isaiah 66:8; Ezekiel 20:42; 37:22)

> **" 'Shall the earth be made to give birth in one day? Or shall a nation be born at once?... Shall I bring to the time of birth, and not cause delivery?' says the Lord."** (Isaiah 66:8, 9)

The United Nations resolution creating Israel also partitioned Jerusalem, with Israel assigned a "Jewish Quarter." During the Six-Day War in 1967, Arab and Jordanian armies attacked Israel and the "Jewish Quarter." Israeli defense forces counterattacked and liberated Jerusalem, bringing the reunited city under Jewish control.[2] This event was a confirmation of the beginning of the end of the **"times of the Gentiles."** (Luke 21:24)

> **"Jerusalem will be trampled by Gentiles until the times of the Gentiles are fulfilled."**

The prophets wrote, **"They** (Jewish people) **shall inherit the land forever....They shall no more be pulled up** (deported) **out of their land which I** (God) **have given them....Foreigners shall no more enslave them....And no one shall make him** (Israel) **afraid."** The present regathering to Israel is **THE FINAL EXODUS**. (Isaiah 60:21; Jeremiah 30:8, 10; Amos 9:15, KJV)

CHAPTER 7

The Last Days

We are warned about the nature of people during these last days:

> **"In the last days perilous times will come: For men will be lovers of themselves, lovers of money, boasters, proud, blasphemers, disobedient to parents, unthankful, unholy, unloving, unforgiving, slanderers, without self-control, brutal, despisers of good, traitors, headstrong, haughty, lovers of pleasure rather than lovers of God....Evil men and impostors will grow worse and worse, deceiving and being deceived..., giving heed to deceiving spirits and doctrines of demons..., swearing, and lying, and killing, and stealing, and committing adultery."**
> (Hosea 4:2, KJV; 1 Timothy 4:1; 2 Timothy 3:1-4, 13)

Many people of this nature occupy elected and appointed positions at all levels of government:

> **"Those who lead you cause you to err.... The prince asks for gifts.... The great man utters his evil desire...which devises evil by law.... Everyone loves bribes..., so they scheme together...and delight in the perversity of the wicked...who call evil good, and good evil...,who receive honor from one another, and do not seek the honor that comes from the only God.... Their judgment and their dignity proceed from themselves.... They will exploit you with deceptive words...and by smooth words and flattering speech deceive the hearts of the simple.... The way of truth will be blasphemed...and their message will spread like cancer.... And many will follow their destructive ways."**
> (Psalm 94:20; Proverbs 2:14; Isaiah 1:23; 3:12; 5:20; Micah 7:3; Habakkuk 1:7; John 5:44; Romans 16:18; 2 Timothy 2:17; 2 Peter 2:2, 3)

When the Israelites rejected God and said, **"Give us a king to judge us,"** God provided Saul as their first king. Citizens today also have free-will choice to select their government, even electing ungodly individuals who will not perform in their best interests. (1 Samuel 8:6)

> **"They do not know, nor do they understand** (the people exploited by deceptive words)**...because they did not receive the**

> **love of the truth.... God will send them a strong delusion,...a spirit of stupor.... For the spirit of harlotry has caused them to stray.... As they did not like to retain God in their knowledge, God gave them over to a debased mind, to do those things which are not fitting..., to their own stubborn heart..., as they have chosen their own ways....They were not deprived of their craving....He gave them their request** (they requested the people elected to office)**; but sent leanness into their soul."** (Psalm 78:30; 81:12; 82:5; 106:15, KJV; Isaiah 66:3; Hosea 4:12; Romans 1:28; 11:8; 2 Thessalonians 2:10, 11)

Because of a lack of spiritual training, pride, selfishness and rebellion reside in adult bodies. Most have no clue about the difference between good and evil. Evil lifestyles are rationalized so that the pain and trauma caused by perverted behaviors are suppressed. People accept politics without principle, seek wealth without work, conduct commerce without ethics, and enjoy pleasure without conscience. Many are embarrassed by those who live by a higher standard of morality. Arrogance and violence are increasing. Anger and fear make them demand that everyone approve of their behavior.

> **"To do evil is like sport to a fool.... The way of a fool is right in his own eyes,... having their own conscience seared with**

> **a hot iron....The bloodthirsty hate the blameless...and he who is upright in the way is an abomination to the wicked.... You** (Jewish people and Christians) **will be hated by all for My name's sake....You will be betrayed even by parents and brothers, relatives and friends.... This is a rebellious people...who will not hear the law of the LORD.... He who is perverse in his ways despises Him** (God)**.... All who desire to live godly...will suffer persecution."** (Proverbs 10:23; 12:15; 14:2; 29:10, 27; Isaiah 30:9; Luke 21:16, 17; 1 Timothy 4:2; 2 Timothy 3:12)

This results in a defective and **"unstable"** mentality: "If you do not approve and support my lifestyle, I will kill you!" (James 1:8)

When Stephen aggravated a small group of people, they **"stoned him."** Adolf Hitler's **"debased mind"** plan, if he had lived, was to eliminate Christians after murdering the Jews.[1] (Acts 7:58; Romans 1:28)

> **"And why did he** (Cain) **murder him** (Abel)? **Because his** (Cain's) **works were evil and his brother's righteous."** (1 John 3:12)

The men of Sodom told Abraham's nephew, Lot, **"We will deal worse with you** (believers in God) **than with them."** (Genesis 19:9)

God knows people and their actions:

> **"Then the LORD saw that the wickedness of**

> **man was great in the earth, and that every intent of the thoughts of his heart was only evil continually.... Men loved darkness rather than light, because their deeds were evil.... They declare their sin as Sodom, they do not hide it."**
> (Genesis 6:5; Isaiah 3:9; John 3:19)

By recognizing evil conduct, we can keep our peace:

> **"Wisdom and knowledge will be the stability of your times.... Since you know these things beforehand, beware lest you also fall from your own steadfastness, being led away with the error of the wicked."**
> (Isaiah 33:6; 2 Peter 3:17)

> **"You** (God) **will keep him in perfect peace, whose mind is stayed on You, because he trusts in You."** (Isaiah 26:3)

PART 4

Relocation

**"Up, Zion! Escape....
Return to the land of your fathers."**

(Genesis 31:3; Zechariah 2:7)

CHAPTER 8

Return to the Land

God directed the ***RELOCATION*** of the children of Israel when He told Jacob to leave Syria after being persecuted by his Gentile father-in-law:

> **"Return to the land of your fathers and to your kindred, and I will be with you."** (Genesis 31:3)

God also told him, **"Your name shall not be called Jacob anymore, but Israel shall be your name."** Israel then returned to the Promised Land with his children born to him in Syria. (Genesis 35:9, 10)

In the years that followed, God judged the land with a famine and Israel took his children to Egypt where Joseph provided for the family. The descendants of Israel's twelve sons later followed Moses out of Egypt to return to the Promised Land.

In later years, prophets and angels conveyed divine instructions to go to the Holy Land:

> **"Flee from the land of the north...**
> **It shall be as the hunted gazelle...;**
> **every man will turn to his own people,**
> **and everyone will flee to his own land...**
> **You who have escaped the sword,**
> **get away! Do not stand still!**
> **Remember the LORD afar off,**
> **and let Jerusalem come to your mind...**
> **Let us go back to our own people**
> **and to the land of our nativity**
> **from the oppressing sword...**
> **And they shall remember Me in far countries;...and they shall return."**
> (Isaiah 13:14; Jeremiah 46:16; 51:50; Zechariah 2:6; 10:9)

Isaiah prophesied that Gentiles would help them move to Israel during a **"second time"** return, meaning after A.D. 70. Isaiah's prophecies are being proven daily as Gentiles are helping them travel to Israel by land, sea and air from countries around the world. (Isaiah 11:11)(See page 28.)

> **"Then people** (Gentiles) **will take them** (Jewish people) **and bring them to their place** (Israel)**...They** (Gentiles) **shall bring your sons in their arms, and your daughters shall be carried on their** (Gentiles') **shoulders...I** (God) **bore you on eagles' wings** (airplanes) **and brought you...And the ships of Tarshish** (large Gentile seagoing vessels) **will bring your sons from afar."** (Exodus 19:4; Isaiah 14:2; 49:22; 60:9)

Jeremiah accurately portrayed the people returning:

> **"I** (God) **will take you, one from a city and two from a family, and I will bring you to Zion.... The blind and the lame, the woman with child,...they shall come with weeping,...trembling from the west."** (Jeremiah 3:14; 31:8, 9; Hosea 11:10)

Some governments stop or deter Jewish movements to Israel. We must pray for those governments to give them **"favor"** and allow them to leave. God exerted pressure on Pharaoh to let the Israelites leave Egypt:

> **"And the Lord gave the people favor in the sight of the Egyptians."** (Exodus 11:3)

Moses wrote that when the Hebrew people were defeated and forced to leave the Holy Land, God would **"bring the land to desolation, and your enemies who dwell in it shall be astonished."** This proved true during the **"seventy years"** of the Babylonian captivity which Jeremiah had prophesied: **"This whole land shall be a desolation....The Lord will change the rain of your land to powder and dust."** (Leviticus 26:32; Deuteronomy 28:24; Jeremiah 25:11)

After the Roman destruction of Jerusalem in A.D. 70, the rains on Israel stopped. Jesus had told them, **"But when you see Jerusalem surrounded..., know that its desolation is near."** The late Mother Basilea Schlink, distinguished author of Jewish history, wrote, "In 1902 the former and latter rains, which had ceased in the first centuries after Christ,...recommenced."[1] (Luke 21:20)

In 1869, Mark Twain, an American writer, wrote in his *Innocents Abroad*, "Jerusalem is mournful, and dreary and lifeless. I would not desire to live there."

Jewish refugees fleeing persecution in Russia were the beginning of the second *Aliyah* (page 28) to the Holy Land from 1882 to 1903.[2] In 1897, the First Zionist Congress in Basel, Switzerland, initiated diplomatic efforts to re-establish a Jewish nation in the Holy Land.[3] In 1902, the former and latter *rains resumed on Israel after more than 1,500 years of drought.*

> **"But you, O mountains of Israel, you shall shoot forth your branches and yield your fruit to MY PEOPLE ISRAEL, FOR THEY ARE ABOUT TO COME** (RETURN)**....He** (God) **will cause the rain to come down... and you** (mountains) **shall be tilled and sown."** (Ezekiel 36:8, 9; Joel 2:23)

> **"This is the sign to you from the LORD, that the LORD will do the thing which He has spoken.... The LORD your God will bless you** (Jewish people) **in the land** (Israel) **which you go to possess."** (Deuteronomy 30:16; 2 Kings 20:9)

> **"As in the days when you came out of the land of Egypt, I** (God) **will show them** (Jewish people) **wonders** (miracles)**."** (Micah 7:15)

> **"You** (God) **will arise and have mercy on Zion; for the time to favor her, yes, *the set time, has come*.... What has been determined shall be done."** (Psalm 102:13; Daniel 11:36)

PART 5

Persecution

"Haman sought to destroy all the Jews who were throughout the whole kingdom..., both young and old, little children and women."

(Esther 3:6, 13)

CHAPTER 9

Hide the Outcasts

Jewish people who do not relocate to Israel are vulnerable to ***PERSECUTION***. It is amazing how the Bible describes the Holocaust and the Islamic terrorists and the "hate groups" of today.

> **"They have despised My people, as if they should no more be a nation before them.... They have said, 'Come, and let us cut them off from being a nation.... The ancient heights have become our possession.... They will neither know nor see anything, till we come into their midst and kill them.'...And all of them conspired together to come and attack Jerusalem and create confusion...and hired counselors against them to frustrate their purpose."** (Ezra 4:5; Nehemiah 4:8, 11; Psalm 83:4; Jeremiah 33:24; Ezekiel 36:2)

> **"Strangers devour your land in your presence.... They revile and persecute you, and say all kinds of evil against you falsely.... Men hate you, and...exclude you.... Whoever kills you will think that he offers God service.... They have also divided up My land...that the name of Israel may be remembered no more."**
> (Psalm 83:4; Isaiah 1:7; Joel 3:2; Matthew 5:11; Luke 6:22; John 16:2)

> **"Haman sought to destroy all the Jews who were throughout the whole kingdom..., both young and old, little children and women."**
> (Esther 3:6, 13)

During the Holocaust, many Jewish families asked for help. They needed to leave the country or find a place to hide. Some gave their children to Gentiles while they hid somewhere else. *We are mandated by the Bible to pray for them and provide for their comfort and safety when they are persecuted:*

> **"Far be it from me that I should sin against the LORD in ceasing to pray for you** (people of Israel)**."** (1 Samuel 12:23)

> **"Pray for the peace of Jerusalem."** (Psalm 122:6).

> **"Open your mouth for the speechless, in the cause of all who are appointed to die."**
> (Proverbs 31:8)

> **" 'Comfort, yes, comfort My people!' says your God. 'Speak comfort to Jerusalem.' "**
> (Isaiah 40:1, 2)

"Do not withhold good from those to whom it is due." (Proverbs 3:27)

"Hide the outcasts, do not betray him who escapes. Let My outcasts dwell with you. Be a shelter to them." (Isaiah 16:3, 4)

"Deliver those who are drawn toward death, and hold back those stumbling to the slaughter. If you say, "Surely we did not know this," does not He who weighs the hearts consider it? He who keeps your soul, does He not know it? And will He not render to each man according to his deeds?" (Proverbs 24:11, 12)

"If you remain completely silent at this time, relief and deliverance will arise for the Jews from another place....Yet who knows whether you have come to the kingdom for such a time as this?" (Esther 4:14)

"If the Gentiles have been partakers of their (the Jews') **spiritual things, their** (the Gentiles') **duty is also to minister to them** (the Jewish people) **in material things."** (Romans 15:27)

Rahab, a Gentile, hid Jewish soldiers and helped them escape from Jericho. (Joshua 2:1-22)

Ebed-Melech, an Ethiopian, saved Jeremiah by rescuing him from a dungeon. (Jeremiah 38:7-13)

Elijah escaped from King Ahab and was sheltered by a Gentile widow in a Gentile nation for three years. (1 Kings 17:8-9)

Ruth, a Gentile, helped her widowed Jewish mother-in-law return to Israel. (Ruth 1:22)

> **"If you know these things, blessed are you if you do them.... Blessed are those who hear the word of God and keep it!"** (Luke 11:28; John 13:17)

God promised to **"bless"** the Jewish people when they are **"in the land** (Israel)**."** This has proven true again during the past century. Blessings began with the miracle of the rainfall in 1902. They include surviving four wars against superior forces, just as Gideon's 300 farmers defeated 135,000 trained troops. We are watching God **"favor"** Israel, **"for at the appointed time the end shall be.... What has been determined shall be done."** (Deuteronomy 30:16; Judges 6-8; Daniel 7:22; 8:19; 11:36)

Any nation oppressing Israel will fail.

> **"No weapon formed against you shall prosper....I** (God) **will contend with him who contends with you....Disaster will come upon them....They shall be as nothing."** (Isaiah 41:11; 49:25; 54:17; Jeremiah 2:3)

Nations supporting enemies of Israel will also fail.

> **"Should you help the wicked and love those who hate the LORD** (God)**? Therefore the wrath of the LORD is upon you....The allies of the proud lie prostrate beneath Him** (God)**."** (2 Chronicles 19:2; Job 9:13)

CHAPTER 10

Touch All That He Has

God's judgment of the United States and anti-Semitic ***PERSECUTION*** may be closer than we realize.

Our government has many high-profile Jewish men and women serving in significant positions of responsibility. They include the present director of the Federal Reserve. If this country experienced a catastrophic economic collapse affecting people's savings and income, it is possible that these individuals and the Jewish community could be blamed even though a collapse has been predicted for years. The Jewish people have been unjustly accused and persecuted for many things over the centuries including the Black Plague in Europe.[1] They are the easiest to accuse, as few people would defend them. An illustration of human reaction to a monetary crisis is given by Satan while talking with God about Job. The devil knew that people become vicious and unstable when their economic status is threatened. He knew they would even blame God for their problems:

> **"You have blessed the work of his hands, and his possessions have increased in the land. But now, stretch out Your hand and touch all that he has, and he will surely curse You to Your face!"... And it shall happen, when they are hungry, that they will be enraged and curse their king** (president) **and their God."**
> (Job 1:10-11; Isaiah 8:21)

The book of Esther shows how a government official reacted when one man made him angry:

> **"Haman sought to destroy all the Jews who were throughout the whole kingdom..., both young and old, little children and women."**
> (Esther 3:6, 13)

The population was prepared to do it in blind obedience because they were not truthfully informed. They depended on their government to tell them what to do.

Adolf Hitler was a type of "Haman." He blamed the Jewish community for problems in Germany and conditioned the German people to accept the Holocaust. Americans have been deceived in the same manner.

How? We have been fed manipulated and false information about Israel by a biased media that is influenced by Islamic stockholders and physical intimidation of reporters in the Holy Land. We have been subjected to degraded values of human life by worldwide violence, riots, death, murder, abortion, euthanasia, suicide, sexual perversion, child abuse, addictions, prison labor, religious persecution, ethnic cleansing, plagues and international terrorism. We have been introduced to large prison systems holding thousands of people. We are surrounded by angry, arrogant and untrustworthy political, judicial, financial and educational officeholders. Islamic extremists and terrorists are accommodated within our borders. We, too, are being conditioned to tolerate abuses of human values and blame someone else for our problems.

THE FINAL EXODUS will have a stunning effect on the United States. Of a total of less than fourteen million Jewish people in the entire world, over five million live in Israel. But almost six million live in the United States.[2] Hosea prophesied that God's chosen people returning to Israel **"shall come trembling from the west** (persecution in the United States and South America)**."** Any attacks on North and South American Jewish communities by resident Islamic terrorists, indigenous "hate groups" or public reaction to events such as an economic collapse, could cause increased migration to Israel. Failure of the United States and others to protect people or facilitate movements to Israel will result in consequences for those countries. (Hosea 11:10)

" 'Comfort, yes, comfort My people!' says your God.... 'Do not withhold good from those who deserve it, when it is in your power to act.... Do not betray him who escapes.... I (God) **will curse him who curses you** (Israel)**. For the nation and kingdom which will not serve you shall perish, and those nations shall be utterly ruined....The Lord will fight for you,...for the battle is not yours, but God's.' "**
(Genesis 12:3; Exodus 14:14; 2 Chronicles 20:15; Proverbs 3:27, NIV; Isaiah 16:3, 40:1, 60:12)

CHAPTER 11

Allegorical Tragedy

For nineteen hundred years, Jewish people have been falsely accused, maligned, ostracized, persecuted, robbed, victimized by crusades, restricted in their religion, denied civil rights, beaten, tortured and murdered, mostly by people claiming to be "Christians." Because of this, many Jewish people resent the cross as a religious symbol and dislike the names "Christian," "Crusade," "Jesus" and "Christ."

These atrocities had their beginning in the third century when an allegorical method involving Greek philosophy was contrived to interpret prophecies in the Scriptures. Up to that time, fulfilled prophecy, including the seventy-year Babylonian captivity and the Crucifixion, occurred as foretold by the literal understanding of Scripture.

> **"The word which I** (God) **speak will come to pass.... It shall not return to Me void."** (Isaiah 55:11; Ezekiel 12:25)

The new allegorical and mystical method promoted the erroneous belief that Jewish people had permanently forfeited God's covenants by rejecting Jesus as their Messiah. It also taught that the Church had "replaced" them in the plan and purpose of God and was the only recipient of the covenants, promises and blessings, but without the judgments. This delusion of denying the people and nation of Israel their unconditional and everlasting promises is the primary motivation for centuries of senseless persecution.[1]

The errors claim the Church, composed of only those acknowledging Jesus, is "New Israel," "True Israel," "Spiritual Israel" and "Israel of God." Only one of these terms, **"Israel of God,"** appears in the Bible, and then only once. There is no other instance in Scripture where "Israel" could be used to mean the Church, and application of this single reference is not accepted unanimously among Bible scholars.[2] Use of any of these terms serves only to reinforce anti-Semitic attitudes and to further alienate the Jewish community. (Galatians 6:16)

Then they were wrongly accused of being "Christ killers." Next came the false assumption that the protection provided by the covenant with Abraham that God would **"curse him who curses you"** no longer applied to them. These led to irresponsible physical attacks without fear of God's judgment. The att started with attempts to force them to embrace Jesu When this failed, they were forced to live outside Gentile communities. Then people regressed to the defective mentality of, "You do not deserve to live, so we will kill you!" This led to millions being murdered for no reason other than being Jewish.[3] Their adversaries said, **"We have not offended, because they have sinned against the LORD."** The killings confirm the warning, **"Whoever kills you will think that he offers God service."** (Genesis 12:3; Jeremiah 50:7; John 16:2)

Incredible as it may seem, propaganda maligning the Jews, such as *The Protocols of the Learned Elders of Zion,* continues to be published in books and on the Internet in many languages. It was produced in 1905 in Russia and claims to reveal the details of a Jewish plot to dominate the world, and has repeatedly been exposed as a concocted forgery intended to legitimatize persecution.[4]

Years of research have also confirmed the deliberate fabrication of false claims that Jewish fighters "massacred" Arab civilians during the battle for the village of Deir Yassin near Jerusalem in April 1948, the month before the Nation of Israel was established. The 1998 report *Deir Yassin: History of a Lie* includes Arab documents never before translated into English. It publishes statements by Arab leaders and eyewitness survivors admitting they fabricated claims of atrocities to encourage Arab regimes to invade the Jewish state-to-be. Arabs have continued to perpetuate this false propaganda

-y years, even erecting a monument
ıe "massacre" that never happened.[5]

ɹiberation Theology" movement that
ationalism within Israel. However, there
is a bi... ımple that invalidates their position when
comparing Jewish captives who returned to Jerusalem from Babylon with Holocaust refugees and other Jews returning to Israel after May 14, 1948.

> **"Now when the adversaries** (non-Jewish) **of Judah and Benjamin heard that the descendants of the captivity were building the temple..., they became very angry...and mocked the Jews.... They troubled them in the building, and hired counselors against them to frustrate their purpose..., and all of them conspired together to come and attack Jerusalem and create confusion."** They said, **"They will neither know nor see anything, till we come into their midst and kill them and cause the work to cease."** (Ezra 4:1, 4-5; Nehemiah 4:1, 7, 8, 11)

The Jewish people in Israel are descendants of the children of Jacob (Israel) whom Moses led out of Egypt. God promised the Holy Land to the **"descendants"** of Abraham, Isaac and Jacob. **"Abraham...dwelt in the land of promise...with Isaac and Jacob, the heirs with him of the same promise."** The land was not promised to Isaac's half brother Ishmael or Jacob's twin brother Esau. **"Abraham gave all that he had** (inheritance) **to Isaac."** The children Abraham had after

Isaac **"he sent...away from Isaac his son, to the country of the east"**; all of them **"have no heritage or right or memorial in Jerusalem."** (Genesis 12:7; 25:5, 6; 26:3; 28:13; Nehemiah 2:20; Hebrews 11:8-9)

God told Jeremiah that some people would wrongly assume God had abandoned His chosen people:

> **"Have you not considered what these people have spoken, saying, 'The two families** (Judah and Israel) **which the LORD has chosen, He has also cast them off?' Thus they have despised My people, as if they should no more be a nation before them. Thus says the LORD: 'If My covenant is not with day and night, and if I have not appointed the ordinances of heaven and earth, then I will cast away the descendants of Jacob and David My servant, so that I will not take any of his descendants to be rulers over the descendants of Abraham, Isaac, and Jacob. For I will cause their captives to return, and will have mercy on them.' "** (Jeremiah 33:24-26)

Do not believe claims without seeking proof. The apostle Paul warns about human philosophy being applied to Scripture interpretation.

> **"Beware lest anyone cheat you through philosophy and empty deceit, according to the tradition of men, according to the basic principles of the world.... God has not cast**

> **away His people** (unbelieving Jews)**.... To provoke them** (unbelieving Jews) **to jealousy, salvation has come to the Gentiles.... If some of the branches were broken off** (unbelieving Jews)**, and you** (believing Gentiles), **being a wild olive tree, were grafted in among them** (believing Jews)**,...do not boast against the branches** (broken off–unbelieving Jews)**. God is able to graft them in again.... But concerning the election they** (unbelieving Jews) **are beloved for the sake of the fathers. For the gifts and the calling of God are irrevocable.... Do not be haughty** (feel superior to unbelieving Jews)**, but fear** (God)**."** (Romans 11:2, 11, 17, 18, 20, 23, 28-29; Colossians 2:8)

> **"For what if some** (Jews) **did not believe? Will their** (the Jews') **unbelief make the faithfulness of God without effect? Certainly not! Indeed, let God be true but every man a liar.... Are we** (believers) **better than they** (unbelieving Jews)**? Not at all."** (Romans 3:3-4, 9)

Hal Lindsey, author of *The Late Great Planet Earth*, wrote in his book *The Road to Holocaust*:

> ***Since the Nation of Israel was elected and created on the basis of pure grace and not human merit, then it cannot be rejected because of human failure.***

PART 6

Believe the Prophets

"O foolish ones, and slow of heart to believe in all that the prophets have spoken!"

"For Zion's sake I will not hold My peace, and for Jerusalem's sake I will not rest."

" 'Comfort, yes, comfort My people!' says your God."

"Will you not declare it?"

(Isaiah 40:1; 48:6; 62:1; Luke 24:25)

CHAPTER 12

People Who Know

There are three categories of prophecy: prophecies fulfilled, such as the **"seventy years"** of Babylonian captivity, prophecies to be fulfilled, which embrace **"the last days,"** and prophecies-in-progress, which include the re-establishment of the Nation of Israel and the regathering of God's chosen people in Israel. (Genesis 49:1; Jeremiah 25:11)

We should be exhilarated to be alive in these times to see "real time" prophecy fulfilled around us!

Scripture tells us:

> **"Scoffers will come in the last says,...saying, 'Where is the promise of His coming? For since the fathers fell asleep, all things continue as they were from the beginning of creation.' "** (2 Peter 3:3)

These scoffers were silenced forever when the Nation of Israel was re-established in 1948. Israel is not only the greatest prophetic miracle since the life of Jesus, but it is a brilliant signpost pointing to **"the end of the days."** (Daniel 12:13)

The current immigration to Israel will be **THE FINAL EXODUS** from foreign nations. God has told them that **"foreigners shall no more enslave them..., they shall no more be pulled up out of their land"** and, therefore, will never be forced to leave the Holy Land again. (Jeremiah 30:8; Amos 9:15, KJV)

We are mandated by God to pray for all the children of Israel, help them return to Israel, and provide for their safety when they are persecuted. We are obeying God when helping them, but not everyone will approve of this service. Opposition, criticism and efforts to stop us should be expected from anti-Semites, churches, friends and even our families. Their lack of knowledge and understanding should not affect our belief, faith and obedience:

> **"O foolish ones, and slow of heart to believe in all that the prophets have spoken!... Do not fear the reproach of men... What is that to you? You follow Me.... People who know their God shall be strong, and carry out great exploits. ...As we have been approved by God to be entrusted with the gospel, even so we speak, not as pleasing men, but God who tests our hearts."** (Isaiah 51:7; Daniel 11:32; Luke 24:25; John 21:22; 1 Thessalonians 2:4)

CHAPTER 13

Do Not Fear

We must trust God for all things in these last days:

> **"Trust in the LORD with all your heart.... Do not be afraid nor dismayed.... Be strong and of good courage.... The battle is not yours, but God's.... I** (God) **will not leave you nor forsake you."** (Joshua 1:5, 6; 2 Chronicles 20:15; Proverbs 3:5)

> **"For God has not given us a spirit of fear, but of power and of love and of a sound mind.... And the peace of God, which surpasses all understanding, will guard your hearts and minds."** (Philippians 4:7; 2 Timothy 1:7)

> **"Blessed is the man who fears the LORD.... He will not be afraid of evil tidings; his heart is steadfast, trusting in the LORD. His**

> **heart is established; he will not be afraid."** (Psalm 112:1, 7-8)

Every miracle in the Bible can be applied to you when you need it. When his sister had leprosy, **"Moses cried out to the Lord..., 'Please heal her, O God, I pray!' "** Peter was sinking in the water and **"cried out..., 'Lord, save me!' "** The Bible confirms God's provision of food and water, shelter, clothing, favorable weather conditions and even money when needed. People were raised from the dead, moved in the Spirit, helped by angels, freed from prison, healed of sickness and disability, saved from fire, protected from animals, revived from beatings, delivered of evil spirits, received supernatural physical strength, information and instructions, and their enemies were temporarily blinded. These miracles confirm that **"with God all things are possible."**
(Numbers 12:13; Matthew 14:30; 19:26)

> **"If you abide in Me, and My words abide in you, you will ask what you desire, and it shall be done for you."** (John 15:7)

> **"Do not fear those who kill the body but cannot kill the soul. But rather fear Him who is able to destroy both soul and body in hell."** (Matthew 10:28)

> **"**(King) **David strengthened himself in the LORD.... For the word of God is living and powerful."** (1 Samuel 30:6; Hebrews 4:12)

Your faith and boldness will be increased when you review the supernatural time line of fulfilled prophecies, many of which you have witnessed.

1. **Roman army captures Jerusalem (A.D. 70)**
   Prophesied by Moses and Jesus
   (See pages 28, 41, 83, 84.)

2. **Israel desolate (after A.D. 70 to 1902)**
   Prophesied by Moses, Jeremiah and Jesus
   There was no rain in the land.
   (See pages 41, 42.)

3. **Second *Aliyah* to Israel begins**
   Prophesied by Moses, Isaiah, Jeremiah, Ezekiel and Zechariah
   (See pages ix, x, 25- 30, 39-42, 48, 83.)

4. **Rain resumes on Israel (1902)**
   Prophesied by Ezekiel
   Miracle of nature
   (See pages 41, 42, 48.)

5. **State of Israel re-established (1948)**
   New home for Holocaust survivors
   People will never be forced to leave.
   (See pages 9, 16, 22, 23, 30, 52, 71, 74.)

6. State of Israel undefeated in four wars

Prophesied by Isaiah, Jeremiah and Amos

Israel will never be defeated again.

(See pages 17, 30, 48, 51, 52, 71, 74.)

7. Gentiles are helping *Aliyah* to Israel

Prophesied by Isaiah and Jeremiah

(See pages ix, x, xiv, 29, 40, 73-80, 87-90.)

CHAPTER 14

They Shall Prosper

When God spoke to Abraham, He promised him:

> **"I will bless those who bless you,
> and I will curse him who curses you;
> and in you all the families of the earth
> shall be blessed."** (Genesis 12:3)

Later, God spoke through Isaac to Jacob:

> **"Cursed be everyone who curses you,
> and blessed be those who bless you!"**
> (Genesis 27:29)

Then He spoke through Balaam for all of Israel:

> **"How lovely are your tents, O Jacob!
> Your dwellings, O Israel!
> Blessed is he who blesses you,
> and cursed is he who curses you."**
> (Numbers 24:5, 9)

King David wrote:

> **"Pray for the peace of Jerusalem: May they prosper who love you."** (Psalm 122:6)

These are illustrations of a faithful God providing blessings to Gentiles who bless His people:

Rahab, a Gentile harlot who *believed in God, hid two Israelite soldiers in her home and helped them escape* from Jericho. *She and her family* were blessed when their lives were spared as the city was captured. She married an Israelite and is named in the genealogy of Jesus. (Joshua 2:1-21; 6:25; Matthew 1:5)

Ruth, a Gentile widow, *helped her Israelite mother-in-law* move from Moab and *return to Israel.* She was blessed by marrying a wealthy landowner, becoming the great-grandmother of King David, and being named in the genealogy of Jesus. (Ruth 1-4; Matthew 1:5)

God told Elijah to leave Israel to the *safety of a Gentile widow's home* in Zarephath, Syria. *The widow and her son* were blessed when God provided their food during a drought and saved them from starvation. (1 Kings 17:8-16)

Ebed-Melech, a king's servant from Ethiopia who *believed in God, saved Jeremiah's life* by rescuing him from a dungeon. God blessed him by sparing his life when Jerusalem was captured. (Jeremiah 38:7-13; 39:15-18)

> A Roman army officer was considered worthy by Jewish elders because he *loved Israel and built a synagogue* for them. He was blessed when *his servant was healed* of a fatal illness. (Luke 7:2-10)

> Cornelius was an Italian soldier who *feared God*, prayed often, and *gave money to Israel's poor people*. An angel told Cornelius to invite Peter into his home. *He and his family* were blessed by being the first Gentiles to believe the word of God and receive the Holy Spirit. (Acts 10:1-6, 34-48)

When God told Abraham, **"I will bless those who bless you,"** He made an everlasting promise to Abraham and all the people of Israel. God performed blessings quickly so Gentiles would recognize they came from God. In the example of Ebed-Melech, the Ethiopian servant, God had Jeremiah tell him his life would be spared so there would be no doubt about the source of the blessing. (Genesis 12:3)

Gentiles are blessed by Jewish people in other ways:

> Laban, the Gentile father-in-law of Jacob, told him, **"The LORD has blessed me for your sake."** (Genesis 30:27)

> Joseph was a slave in Egypt, and **"the LORD blessed the Egyptian's house for Joseph's sake."** (Genesis 39:5)

Ten percent (10%) of the recipients of a Nobel Prize have been Jewish, yet they comprise less than one-half of one percent (0.5%) of the world's population.[1] God told Abraham, **"In you all the families of the earth shall be blessed."** (Genesis 12:2, 3)

Derek Prince, international teacher and author, stated:

> I have discovered that making a commitment of this kind to pray for Jerusalem and Israel will definitely stir up a special measure of opposition from satanically inspired forces. On the other hand, I have also discovered that God's promise given to those who do pray in this way will hold true–**"they shall prosper that love thee."** This is a scriptural pathway to prosperity–not merely in a financial or material sense, but as embracing an abiding assurance of God's favor, provision and protection.[2] (Psalm 122:6, KJV)

Scripture proves people who help Israel see increased blessings very quickly. When we pray for the peace of Jerusalem, Israel and its people, and send them money or perform a service for them, we are obedient to God and will receive a God-given increased love for Israel.

Everyone enjoys blessings from God, but most people do not want to hear about curses. When God told Abraham, Isaac and Balaam, **"I will curse him who curses you....Cursed be everyone who curses you....Cursed is he who curses you** (Israel)." He was not speaking idle words. **"My word...shall not return to Me void."** (Genesis 12:3; 27:29; Numbers 24:9; Isaiah 55:11)

When Hagar, an Egyptian Gentile, **"despised"** her mistress Sarah whom God had chosen to be the mother of Isaac, she was expelled from Abraham's camp along with her teenage son, Ishmael. He had learned his mother's attitude and was publicly **"scoffing"** Isaac. Their chastisement was expulsion for cursing God's chosen people both silently and openly. (Genesis 16:4, 5; 21:8, 9)

God has also declared international chastisement of Gentile nations for cursing the Nation of Israel:

> **"All those who are incensed against you** (Israel) **shall be ashamed and disgraced; they shall be as nothing, and those who strive with you shall perish. For the nation and kingdom which will not serve you shall perish, and those nations shall be utterly ruined."** (Isaiah 41:11; 60:12)

Job understood that people do not curse people:

> **"I have not allowed my mouth to sin by asking for a curse on his soul."** (Job 31:30)

We will do well to remember:

> **"God is not mocked.... You shall not curse the people** (children of Israel)**, for they are blessed."** (Numbers 22:12; Galatians 6:7)

CHAPTER 15

We Must Stand

We must stand with God's people or fall alone. We must stand up and do what we are able before it is too late to do anything. The possibility of Jewish persecution in the United States cannot be ignored. Christians and Jews in China, Africa, South America, Europe and the Middle East are being oppressed, imprisoned, tortured and murdered. Sixty years ago, these actions were a prelude to the Holocaust in Europe. Today, most people do nothing but watch these atrocities as they did then. These "watchers" are like Lot's sons-in-law who thought he was **"joking"** when he warned them that Sodom would be destroyed. Years later, Jesus called them, **"Hypocrites! You know how to discern the face of the sky, but you cannot discern the signs of the times."** (Genesis 19:14; Matthew 16:3)

God has spoken clearly about Israel:

> **"I am the LORD your God.**
> **I have chosen you.**
> **I will not leave you nor forsake you.**
> **I will strengthen you, yes, I will help you.**
> ***The LORD Your God will bless you in the land***
> **I will make them one nation**
> **And no longer shall they be pulled up**
> (defeated)." (Exodus 6:7; Deuteronomy 30:16;
> Joshua 1:5; Isaiah 41:9-10; Ezekiel 37:22;
> Amos 9:15)

God also knows the foolishness of men:

> **"The kings of the earth set themselves,**
> **and the rulers take counsel together....**
> **They have said, 'Come, and let us cut them**
> (Israel) **off from being a nation'**
> **He** (God) **who sits in heaven shall laugh...**
> **'I** (God) **will curse him who curses you** (Israel).
> **And those who strive with you shall perish.**
> **Then they shall know that I am the LORD.' "**
> (Genesis 12:3; Psalm 2:2, 4; 83:4; Isaiah 41:11;
> Ezekiel 36:38)

Anti-Semitism is again escalating rapidly throughout the globe and may challenge our way of life very soon. In recent years, many individuals in the United States have been inspired to make provisions to help Jewish people expected to flee to Israel from persecution in this country. This is not a new phenomenon. From

1974 through to 1991, inspired individuals in Europe were preparing to help the Jewish population of the Soviet Union move through Europe to Israel.[1]

When the Jewish Exodus began in 1991, many of the immigrants benefited from these preparations, particularly in Finland. Some of these individuals were also instrumental in creating Christian organizations in the former Soviet Union that have helped thousands of immigrants move to Israel in the past ten years.[2] There is no doubt that we are witnessing **THE FINAL EXODUS** of God's chosen people to their Promised Land.

King Solomon's prophetic admonition has great significance:

> **"Deliver those who are drawn toward death, and hold back those stumbling to the slaughter. If you say, 'Surely we did not know this,' does not He who weighs the hearts consider it? He who keeps your soul, does He not know it? And will He not render to each man according to his deeds?"** (Proverbs 24:11-12)

We are in the ***WARNING*** and ***RELOCATION*** phases of **THE FINAL EXODUS.** ***PERSECUTION*** is already visible in many countries but is not adequately reported by the media. A 50th anniversary celebration of the Nation of Israel attended by thousands of Christians in Orlando, Florida, during

May 1998, affirmed a statement that every person should endorse:

> **I hereby commit myself to view any anti-Semitic act against a Jewish person, group, business, institution or synagogue as an act against my own church and when I become aware of such anti-Semitism in my community, to actively oppose and condemn it, individually and corporately with others by every means possible.**[3]

The State of Israel's Law of Return allows any person who has Jewish parents or grandparents to "return" to Israel and become a citizen without losing their United States citizenship. Jewish heritage must be established by family or synagogue records, or other information acceptable to the Israeli government.

We must help all Jewish people move to Israel regardless of their nationality or religious beliefs. Prayers for them are most important. They also need encouragement to relocate, which could include assistance to obtain passports and travel tickets. They may require financial aid and living accommodations prior to departure, transportation to the airport or seaport, and protection if escaping persecution. King David was advised to **"stay in a secret place and hide."** The apostle Paul asked for help: **"For I hope to see you on my journey, and to be helped on my way there by you."** (1 Samuel 19:2; Romans 15:24)

Everyone should have a passport to be able to travel quickly. Encourage Jewish friends and acquaintances to obtain a passport or renew their passport if it is close to the expiration date. U.S. citizens only need a passport and travel ticket to go to Israel. They will receive a ninety (90)-day tourist visa upon arrival in Israel and can file other documents during the visa period.

Applications for U.S. passports are available from the U.S. Postal Service, county courthouse or possibly a travel agent. Minor children may be included on an adult passport, but it is better to have a separate passport for each family member.

Visiting the rabbi of a local synagogue may develop future opportunities to be helpful. We can also contact Jewish friends in our neighborhood and workplace to offer them help and protection if needed.

We can work with local churches to promote prayer for Israel while teaching God's plan for Israel and the Jewish heritage of the Church. This will increase God's blessings on those churches.

If we help Jewish and Christian organizations focusing on relocation and resettlement of Jewish immigrants to Israel, it will demonstrate our willingness to do more than just talk about our love for Israel. Cornerstone Church in San Antonio, Texas, contributed over one million dollars to the United Jewish Appeal in 1998 for airline tickets to transport immigrants to Israel from the former Soviet Union. Our duty **"is also to minister to them in material things."** (Romans 15:27)

There are non-Jewish organizations in the former Soviet Union listed on pages 87-90. They locate and assist poorer people who do not know relocation procedures and lack money to acquire documents for their international passport, Israeli visa and final bus or train transportation to the airport or seaport.

They also provide humanitarian aid and living expenses during the three to six months needed to obtain documents, travel to government offices, and wait for document approvals before moving to Israel.

These organizations are extending operations into Latin America. The Jewish Agency for Israel has established offices in Argentina to provide resettlement assistance and free transportation for immigrants to Israel. Non-Jewish relocation organizations work with the Agency by providing services to low income immigrants in the former Soviet Union, and are prepared to continue this assistance wherever needed.

> **"I** (God) **will lift up mine hand to the Gentiles,... and they shall bring thy** (Jewish) **sons in their arms, and thy** (Jewish) **daughters shall be carried upon their shoulders."** (Isaiah 49:22, KJV)

We can oppose anti-Jewish and anti-Christian situations by contacting elected officials and writing newspaper, television and radio media. This could influence changes and will always be an encouragement to the people involved. It is also an example to others who are less informed or hesitant to respond. I visited a concentration camp in Germany and will always remember the feeling of oppression I had while walking through the gas chamber and the shock of seeing the row of rusty furnaces used to burn up the bodies of those who had been murdered.

Visiting a Holocaust center will expand your understanding of anti-Semitism and give you a firm base to refute revisionist lies that the Holocaust never occurred. The United States Holocaust Memorial Museum, 100 Raoul Wallenberg Place, SW, Washington, DC 20024-2150; website www.ushmm.org; has exhibits and a bookstore that will have a profound impact on your life. Another excellent source of information is the Simon Wiesenthal Center in Los Angeles, CA; website www.wiesenthal.com.

Involvement with the Jewish community will open up opportunities to demonstrate our love and care for them as God's chosen people. During these times, we should ask them to forgive us. The United States has anti-Jewish attitudes and has failed to help many times. We also tolerate non-Americans conducting anti-Jewish activities in this country. Daniel set the example when he prayed for God to forgive him and **"all Israel"** as a nation for their sins. We need to pray as Daniel did and ask for forgiveness and to be reconciled with those affected by our national and personal sins. (Daniel 9:4-18)

We must recognize the wisdom of Mordecai:

> **"Do not think in your heart that you will escape.... If you remain completely silent at this time, relief and deliverance will arise for the Jews from another place, but you and your father's house will perish. Yet who knows whether you have come to the kingdom for such a time as this?"** (Esther 4:13, 14)

PART
7

Pursue Peace

"For God is not the author of confusion but of peace"

(1 Corinthians 14:33)

CHAPTER 16

Take Heed

The destruction of Jerusalem in A.D. 70, followed by deportation of the Jewish people throughout the Gentile nations, and their continuing return to Israel this past century, was prophesied by Moses shortly before he died in the wilderness.

"They (Romans) **shall besiege you at all your gates** (Jerusalem)**.... Then the LORD will scatter you among all peoples, from one end of the earth to the other,...back to Egypt in ships,...as male and female slaves.... Now it will come to pass...that the LORD your God will bring you back...*again*** (second *Aliyah*, page 28) **from all the nations where the LORD your God has scattered you...and have compassion on you...that you may dwell in the land** (Israel) **which the LORD swore to your fathers, to Abraham, Isaac, and Jacob."** (Deuteronomy 28:52, 64, 68; 30:1, 3, 20)

Jesus was visiting Jerusalem in A.D. 29 when He prophesied the city's destruction by the Romans:

> **"For days will come upon you** (Jerusalem) **when your enemies will build an embankment around you, surround you and close you in on every side....And Jerusalem will be trampled by Gentiles until the times of the Gentiles are fulfilled."**
> (Luke 19:43; 21:24)

These prophecies by Moses and Jesus were understood by the literal interpretation of Scripture. The normal meaning of the words, grammar and context speaks for itself, and was the method used by the apostles and early Church leaders.[1]

Unfortunately, some churches use an allegorical interpretation of Scripture to justify "Replacement Theology," which is discussed in Chapter 11. These interpretations claim that the Church "replaces" the Jewish people as the chosen people of God.

The historically proven literal interpretation of Scripture also foretells God's people returning to Israel. Many advocates of "Replacement Theology" do not recognize the second reestablishment of Israel in 1948 as one of the **"signs of the times"** that started "God's time clock" for the countdown to **"the time of the end."** The existence of Israel as a nation and the continuing immigration to Israel are literal fulfillments of prophecies that prove the Bible is true. (Daniel 8:17; Matthew 16:3)

These churches do not declare **"the whole counsel of God,"** which speaks of God's faithfulness to His promises to the Jewish people and His plan and purpose for Israel. They **"have neglected"** the truth of the Church's Jewish heritage, the blessings received from helping His people and Israel, and the consequences of cursing them by rejecting and refusing to help them. They fail to realize that God's faithfulness to His promises to the Church is dependent upon His faithfulness to His promises to Israel. The lack of these teachings leaves people confused and unprepared for prophecy-in-progress events, while creating and reinforcing anti-Semitism due to their **"lack of knowledge."** (Hosea 4:6; Matthew 23:23; Acts 20:27)

Hal Lindsey, author of *The Late Great Planet Earth*, one of the best-selling books in history, wrote in his book *The Road to Holocaust* that God's election of Israel is the same as His election of individuals. In fact, God's dealing with Israel as a nation is a picture of how He deals with us as individuals. ***Since the Nation of Israel was elected and created on the basis of pure grace and not human merit, then it cannot be rejected because of human failure.***[2] We must remember **"that the gifts and the calling of God are irrevocable."** (Romans 11:29)

"Replacement Theology" is unnecessary! Individual believing Gentiles **"are all sons of God through faith.... Those who are of faith are sons of Abraham..., Abraham's seed, and heirs according to the promise..., blessed with believing**

Abraham." We receive these blessings by God's **"grace,"** not by "replacing" His people. We have nothing to gain by "replacing" anyone, especially the chosen people of God. (Galatians 3:7, 9, 26, 29; Ephesians 2:8)

Many pastors and teachers learn "Replacement Theology" in liberal seminaries, and most would not consider themselves anti-Semitic. However, we are warned about erroneous teaching:

> **"Take heed what you hear..., that no one deceives you.... Those who lead you cause you to err."... And those who are led by them are destroyed."** (Isaiah 3:12; 9:16; Matthew 24:4; Mark 4:24)

We need to be aware of what is being taught by liberal theologians and college teachers of religion. We must pray that teachers and people who are deceived by "Replacement Theology" will **"come to the knowledge of the truth.... For God is not the author of confusion but of peace."** (1 Corinthians 14:33; 2 Timothy 3:7)

> **"But you must continue in the things which you have learned and been assured of, knowing from whom you have learned them.... Read what was spoken to you by God"** in the Bible. (Matthew 22:31; 2 Timothy 3:14)

Relocation and Resettlement

The State of Israel allows Jewish immigrants to "return" to Israel from any country in the world. People moving to Israel from the twelve countries of the former Soviet Union must obtain an international passport from their government. This usually involves traveling long distances to government offices and payment of debts before the passport will be issued.

After receiving an international passport, they must go to an Israeli embassy or consulate to obtain a visa to Israel. The embassy will require certificates of birth, marriage, religious ceremonies or other documents to prove their Jewish heritage. The government of Israel prohibits the granting of a visa for Jewish immigrants who are members of another religion.

After receiving a visa, most travelers go to an office of the Jewish Agency for Israel. The Agency provides them free airline tickets to Israel. Over one million of an estimated three million eligible immigrants in the former Soviet Union have moved to Israel, mostly by air transportation.

Christian organizations from England, Israel, the Netherlands, Sweden and the United States, mostly staffed by volunteers and all supported by private financial contributions, are in the former Soviet Union to help immigrants move to Israel. This land area is nearly three times as large as the continental United States, and has eleven time zones between the former 6,000 mile east-west borders. Traveling involves extremely cold weather during the winter, unreliable bus transportation over hazardous roads for hundreds of miles, highway bandits, and long train rides which often require changing trains.

These agencies locate people, often in remote communities, and help them assemble documents (when obtainable) from distant locations, arrange their travel to apply for passports, visas and tickets, and help them move to an airport. They also pay for documents and debts. Processing requires several months and costs can exceed $350 per person. Throughout this period, they often provide living expenses, food, clothing, housing, medical and dental supplies, job training and special arrangements for street children and orphans. All services are provided without attempting to evangelize the immigrants.

The International Christian Embassy Jerusalem (Jerusalem, Israel) is the pioneer in helping people move to Israel. The Embassy's main operation in the former Soviet Union is the "Russian Connection" involving air transportation through St. Petersburg, Russia, and Helsinki, Finland. They also operate the Raoul Wallenberg Centre in Budapest, Hungary, and joint-venture with other organizations in Novosibirsk, Russia, which is the gateway to Siberia.

Ezra International assists the "poorest of the poor" immigrants including physically impaired, elderly, homeless, street children and orphans. They meet with church, synagogue and community leaders to inform them of the services available for moving to Israel, and to enlist their assistance in contacting and helping Jewish residents in their areas. When necessary, Ezra arranges for special housing in Israel for the elderly who would otherwise be denied an Israeli visa. They also provide feeding programs for impoverished families over the many months of waiting for their documents.

Immigrants arriving in Israel receive settlement assistance from the Israeli government and many international Christian and Jewish organizations. Bridges for Peace is one of the oldest American humanitarian aid agencies in Israel and is working together with Ezra International, the International Christian Embassy Jerusalem, The Jerusalem Connection International, Ebenezer Emergency Fund, and Ministry to Israel. These cooperative efforts enable people to move and be resettled more efficiently than if all functions were performed by a single organization.

Relocation Organizations

Bridges for Peace
PO Box 33145
Tulsa, OK 74153-1145
www.bridgesforpeace.com

Ebenezer Emergency Fund USA
PO Box 188
Spring Brook, NY 14140-0188
www.ebenezerusa.org

Ezra International
PO Box 120926
Clermont, FL 34712-0926
www.ezrausa.org

International Christian Embassy Jerusalem
PO Box 39255
Washington, DC 20016
www.icej.org

Ministry to Israel
PO Box 4431
Cleveland, TN 37320
www.ministrytoisrael.com

The Jerusalem Connection International
PO Box 20295
Washington, DC 20041
www.tjci.org

Notes

B.C. dates: Edward Reese, *The Reese Chronological Bible* (Minneapolis, MN: Bethany House, 1980).

Chapter 2: The Chosen People

1. John Hagee, *Prophecy Study Bible* (Nashville, TN: Thomas Nelson, 1997), p. 226.

Chapter 3: The Promised Land

1. Israel's Jubilee Conference, 1998 Program Book,(Jacksonville Beach, FL: The Christian Alliance for Israel, 1998), p. 45.
2. Ibid., pp. 45, 48.

Chapter 4: Sarah's Only Son

1. John Hagee, *Beginning of the End* (Nashville, TN: Thomas Nelson, 1996), pp. 24-28.

Chapter 5: The Flood

1. Clarence L. Barnhart, *The World Book Dictionary* (Field Enterprises Educational Corp., 1974), p. 1001.

Chapter 6: Escape for Your Life

1. Michael L. Brown, *Our Hands Are Stained With Blood* (Shippensburg, PA: Destiny Image, 1996), pp. 149-150.
2. Howard M. Sachar, *A History of Israel* (New York, NY: Alfred A. Knopf, 1985), pp. 643-645, 650-655.

Chapter 7: The Last Days

1. Daniel Goldhagen, *Hitler's Willing Executioners* (New York, NY: Vintage Books, 1996), pp. 118, 447-448.

Chapter 8: Return to the Land

1. Basilea Schlink, *Israel, My Chosen People* (Harpenden, Herts, U.K.: Kanaan Publications, 1995), p. 94.
2. *A History of Israel*, pp. 26-32.
3. Ibid., pp. 44-47.

Chapter 10: Touch All That He Has

1. Hal Lindsey, *The Road to Holocaust* (New York, NY: Bantam Books, 1989), pp. 21-22.
2. The American Jewish Committee, *American Jewish Year Book 2000* (New York, NY: The American Jewish Committee, 2000), pp. 242, 247.

Chapter 11: Allegorical Tragedy

1. John Hagee, *Final Dawn Over Jerusalem* (Nashville, TN: Thomas Nelson, 1998), pp. 97-98.
2. *The Road to Holocaust*, pp. 8-9, 267-269.
3. Ibid., pp. 2-3, 6-8, 24-25.
4. Rabbi Abraham Cooper, "Protocols" Memorandum (Los Angeles, CA: Simon Wiesenthal Center, 1998).
5. Morton A. Klein, *Deir Yassin: History of a Lie* (New York, NY: Zionist Organization of America, 1998), pp. 5, 21, 26-27, 33.

Chapter 14: They Shall Prosper

1. Ralph W. Harris, *Thank God for the Jews* (Springfield, MO: *Pentecostal Evangel*, Dec. 25, 1994).
2. Derek Prince, *Our Debt to Israel* (Fort Lauderdale, FL: Derek Prince Ministries).

Chapter 15: We Must Stand

1. Steve Lightle, *Exodus II* (Kingwood, TX: Hunter Books, 1983) pp. 66-75, 91-93.
2. Steve Lightle, *Operation Exodus II* (Tulsa, OK: Insight Publishing, 1998), pp. 174-187.
3. The Christian Alliance for Israel, Special Handout.

Chapter 16: Take Heed

1. *The Road to Holocaust*, pp. 74, 77.
2. Ibid., p. 141.

Bibliography

Literal and allegorical interpretations of Scripture are discussed by John Hagee in *Final Dawn Over Jerusalem,* and by Michael L. Brown in *Our Hands Are Stained With Blood.* Practical experiences for helping people are found in *Sheltering the Jews,* by Mordecai Paldiel, and in *The Hiding Place,* by Corrie ten Boom.

American Jewish Committee. *American Jewish Year Book 2000.* Scranton, PA: Haddon Craftsmen, 2000.

Brown, Michael M. *Our Hands Are Stained With Blood.* Shippensburg, PA: Destiny Image, 1992.

Dobson, Ed. *The End.* Grand Rapids, MI: Zondervan, 1997.

Goldhagen, Daniel Jonah. *Hitler's Willing Executioners.* New York, NY: Vintage Books, 1996.

Hagee, John. *Beginning of the End.* Nashville, TN: Thomas Nelson, 1996.

Hagee, John. *Final Dawn Over Jerusalem.* Nashville,TN: Thomas Nelson, 1998.

Hagee, John. *Prophecy Study Bible.* Nashville, TN: Thomas Nelson, 1997.

Hess, Tom. *Let My People Go!* 2nd ed. Washington, DC: Progressive Vision, 1988.

Klein, Morton A. *Deir Yassin: History of a Lie.* New York, NY: Zionist Organization of America, 1998.

Lambert, Lance. *Israel–The Unique Land–The Unique People.* Wheaton, IL: Tyndale House, 1981.

Lightle, Steve. *Exodus II.* Kingwood, TX: Hunter Books, 1983.

Lightle, Steve. *Operation Exodus II.* Tulsa, OK: Insight Publishing, 1998.

Lindsey, Hal. *Apocalypse Code.* Palos Verdes, CA: Western Front, 1997.

Lindsey, Hal. *Planet Earth–2000 A.D. revised updated ed.* Palos Verdes, CA: Western Front, 1996.

Lindsey, Hal. *The Road to Holocaust.* New York, NY: Bantam Books, 1989.

McQuaid, Elwood. *The Zion Connection.* Eugene, OR: Harvest House, 1996.

Morris, Henry M. *The Genesis Record.* Grand Rapids, MI: Baker Book House, 1990.

Paldiel, Mordecai. *Sheltering the Jews–Stories of Holocaust Rescuers.* Minneapolis, MN: Fortress Press, 1996.

Prince, Derek. *Our Debt to Israel.* Fort Lauderdale, FL: Derek Prince Ministries, undated.

Sachar, Howard M. *A History of Israel.* New York, NY: Alfred A. Knopf, 1985.

Schlink, Basilea. *Israel, My Chosen People.* Harpenden, Herts, U.K.: Kanaan, 1995.

Sumrall, Lester. *Jerusalem–Where Empires Die.* Nashville, TN: Thomas Nelson, 1984.

Ten Boom, Corrie. *The Hiding Place.* Old Tappan, NJ: Fleming H. Revell, 1971.

Wiesel, Elie. *Night.* New York, NY: Bantam Books, 1982.

Wilkerson, David. *America's Last Call.* Lindale, TX: Wilkerson Trust, 1998.

Wilson, Marvin R. *Our Father Abraham.* Grand Rapids, MI: William B. Eerdmans, 1997.

About the Author

William Carr Blood was born at home in East Rochester, New York, and resides in Orlando, Florida, with his wife, Dorothy.

After a twenty-year career as an officer in the United States Army, he worked with railroad, seaport, airport and international trade industries. He attended North Georgia College, graduated from the University of Maryland, and is a Certified Member of the American Society of Transportation and Logistics (Emeritus) and former director of the National Association of Foreign-Trade Zones.

The Final Exodus has been published in Russian and translated into Spanish. His first book, *Miracles!* has also been published in Russian and translated into Chinese and Spanish.